DETROIT TIGERS
ALL-TIME GREATS

BY ETHAN OLSON

Book design by Jake Slavik
Cover design by Jake Slavik

Photographs ©: Mark Duncan/AP Images, cover (top), 1 (top); AP Images, cover (bottom), 1 (bottom); Mark Rucker/Transcendental Graphics/Getty Images Sport/Getty Images, 4, 7, 9; Bettmann/Getty Images, 10; Focus on Sport/Getty Images Sport/Getty Images, 13, 14, 16; Chris Covatta/Getty Images Sport/Getty Images, 18; Ezra Shaw/Getty Images Sport/Getty Images, 20

Press Box Books, an imprint of Press Room Editions.

ISBN
978-1-63494-796-1 (library bound)
978-1-63494-816-6 (paperback)
978-1-63494-854-8 (epub)
978-1-63494-836-4 (hosted ebook)

Library of Congress Control Number: 2023910381

Distributed by North Star Editions, Inc.
2297 Waters Drive
Mendota Heights, MN 55120
www.northstareditions.com

Printed in the United States of America
012024

ABOUT THE AUTHOR

Ethan Olson is a sportswriter and editor based in Minneapolis.

TABLE OF CONTENTS

COBB

CHAPTER 1
DETROIT DOMINANCE

The Detroit Tigers played their first season in 1901. The team struggled for a few years. But that changed when **Ty Cobb** joined the Tigers in 1905.

The center fielder's competitive spirit was unmatched, especially at the plate. During his 22 seasons with Detroit, Cobb set more than 90 Major League Baseball (MLB) records. That included his career batting average of .366 and 12 American League (AL) batting titles.

While Cobb was versatile, right fielder **Sam Crawford** was a pure slugger. He and Cobb had an intense rivalry that pushed both Detroit stars to get even better. That competitiveness helped Crawford lead the AL in home runs twice and runs batted in (RBIs) three times with the Tigers.

Meanwhile, **George Mullin** held down the defensive side with consistent pitching. In 1909, he went on an elite run. Mullin started the season 11–0, a team record that stood for 104 years. He finished the 1909 season with a league-high 29 wins and a career-low 2.22 earned run average (ERA). That helped Detroit earn its third straight AL pennant. However, the Tigers lost in the World Series each year.

STAT SPOTLIGHT

CAREER HITS

TIGERS TEAM RECORD

Ty Cobb: 3,900

Soon, a new group of stars arrived in Detroit. **Harry Heilmann** took off after permanently switching to right field in 1921. He led the AL with 237 hits that year and won the first of his four AL batting titles.

Charlie Gehringer joined the Tigers in 1924. The "Mechanical Man" was known as one of the best second basemen of his era. Hall of Fame shortstop Joe Sewell once said, "I couldn't hit a ball past him. . . . He'd just coast around that infield, just like somebody skating."

Detroit made it back to the World Series in 1934 and 1935. The Tigers lost again in 1934, but the next year was a different story. First baseman **Hank Greenberg** won the AL Most Valuable Player (MVP) Award in 1935, leading the league in home runs and RBIs. And the Tigers beat the Chicago Cubs in six games to win their first championship.

A SPECIAL HOME

Tiger Stadium was the home of the Detroit Tigers from 1912 until 1999. When the park was expanded in 1936, the second-level deck reached above the outfield fence. This sometimes led to fly balls ending up as home runs, as the deck would catch the ball before any outfielder could.

GREENBERG
5

KALINE
6

CHAPTER 2
GLORY DAYS AGAIN

The Detroit Tigers remained a strong team after the 1935 title. **Hal Newhouser** blossomed into a major star in Detroit. The lefty won the AL MVP Award in 1944 and 1945. And he won two games in the 1945 World Series to help the Tigers win another championship.

A new era of Detroit baseball was led by **Al Kaline** after he debuted in 1953. The right fielder went straight from high school to MLB and excelled right away. As a 20-year-old in 1955, he became the youngest player in MLB history to win a batting title. "Mr. Tiger" would go on to play 22 seasons with Detroit.

While Kaline went pro right out of high school, **Norm Cash** didn't play baseball until college. The first baseman grew up farming and got his strength from driving a tractor. That's how Cash was able to hit 373 home runs with the Tigers.

Along with Cash came Detroit native **Bill Freehan**. The catcher earned All-Star honors 11 times in his 15-year career. Freehan's best season came in 1968. That year, he posted career highs in home runs and RBIs. More importantly, he was a defensive force for one of the best pitching teams in baseball.

STAT SPOTLIGHT

CAREER HOME RUNS

TIGERS TEAM RECORD

Al Kaline: 399

Both **Denny McLain** and **Mickey Lolich** entered the rotation in 1963. Together they made one of the most feared pitching combinations in the league. McLain was outspoken about his talents, and he backed it up on the mound. In 1968, the righty became the first MLB pitcher in 34 years to win 30 or more games in a season. That earned him the AL MVP and Cy Young awards. The Cy Young is given to the best pitcher in each league.

McLAIN
17

McLain was Detroit's biggest star in 1968. But Lolich became Detroit's hero in that year's World Series. The Tigers faced the defending champion St. Louis Cardinals. Lolich pitched three complete games, including the series-clinching Game 7, to make the Tigers champions again. For his performance, Lolich won the World Series MVP Award.

That duo continued to thrive with Detroit. McLain tossed nine shutouts in 1969 and won the AL Cy Young again. Starting in 1969, Lolich struck out at least 200 batters per season for six years straight.

THE BIRD

Mark Fidrych didn't play long for Detroit. But his personality made him a fan favorite. Known as "The Bird" because he resembled Big Bird from *Sesame Street*, the pitcher would talk to himself or the ball during games. Sometimes Fidrych refused to use certain balls, insisting they "had hits in them." He asked for them to be removed from the game.

MORRIS
47

CHAPTER 3

RETURN OF THE TIGERS

The Tigers saw three future stars debut in 1977. **Jack Morris** was one of them. The righty was an intense competitor. Longtime Detroit manager Sparky Anderson said he was scared to go to the mound to take Morris out of a game.

Lou Whitaker was a top prospect at third base. But the Tigers moved him to second base to play alongside shortstop **Alan Trammell**. Their chemistry made them one of the best double-play combinations in MLB history. The duo manned the middle infield in Detroit for 19 seasons.

Morris, Whitaker, and Trammell led the Tigers to the 1984 World Series. Against his hometown San Diego Padres, Trammell hit .450 in the series. In Game 4, he belted a pair of home runs that drove in all four of Detroit's runs. The Tigers won the series in five games, and Trammell won the World Series MVP Award.

The Tigers went into a long slump shortly after 1984. However, things started to turn around when **Justin Verlander** made his debut in 2005. The righty dominated hitters with his velocity. Verlander went on to lead the AL in strikeouts in four different seasons with Detroit. One of those seasons was 2011, when he won the AL MVP and Cy Young awards. Over time, Verlander became known as one of the best pitchers of his era.

Just behind him in the rotation was righty **Max Scherzer**. "Mad Max" had an intense personality. But he was always focused on the mound. On June 28, 2013, Scherzer broke George Mullin's 104-year-old record by

NEAR PERFECTION

On June 2, 2010, Detroit's Armando Galarraga was on the verge of history against the Cleveland Indians. With one more out needed to throw a perfect game, umpire Jim Joyce incorrectly ruled that a Cleveland batter made it to first safely. Joyce later realized his mistake. After the game, Joyce was in tears when he apologized to Galarraga. The pitcher understood and told reporters, "Nobody's perfect."

CABRERA
24

starting the season 12–0. That same year, he was rewarded with an AL Cy Young Award of his own.

Infielder **Miguel Cabrera** consistently provided run support for Verlander and Scherzer. That was never truer than in 2012, as Cabrera hit for the first Triple Crown in 45 years. That is when a player leads the league in batting average, home runs, and RBIs.

By 2018, Verlander and Scherzer were both on different teams. However, Cabrera stayed in Detroit. The two-time MVP recorded his 500th home run and 3,000th hit with the Tigers.

STAT SPOTLIGHT

CAREER WIN-LOSS PERCENTAGE

TIGERS TEAM RECORD

Max Scherzer: .701

TIMELINE

1901
GEORGE MULLIN
(1902–13)
1910
SAM CRAWFORD
(1903–17)
TY COBB
(1905–26)
1920
HARRY HEILMANN
(1914, 1916–29)
1930
CHARLIE GEHRINGER
(1924–42)
HANK GREENBERG
(1930, 1933–41, 1945–46)
1940
HAL NEWHOUSER
(1939–53)
1950
AL KALINE
(1953–74)
1960
NORM CASH
(1960–74)
BILL FREEHAN
(1961, 1963–76)
DENNY McLAIN
(1963–70)
1970
MICKEY LOLICH
(1963–75)
1980
JACK MORRIS
(1977–90)
LOU WHITAKER
(1977–95)
1990
ALAN TRAMMELL
(1977–96)
2000
JUSTIN VERLANDER
(2005–17)
2010
MAX SCHERZER
(2010–14)
MIGUEL CABRERA
(2008–)
2020

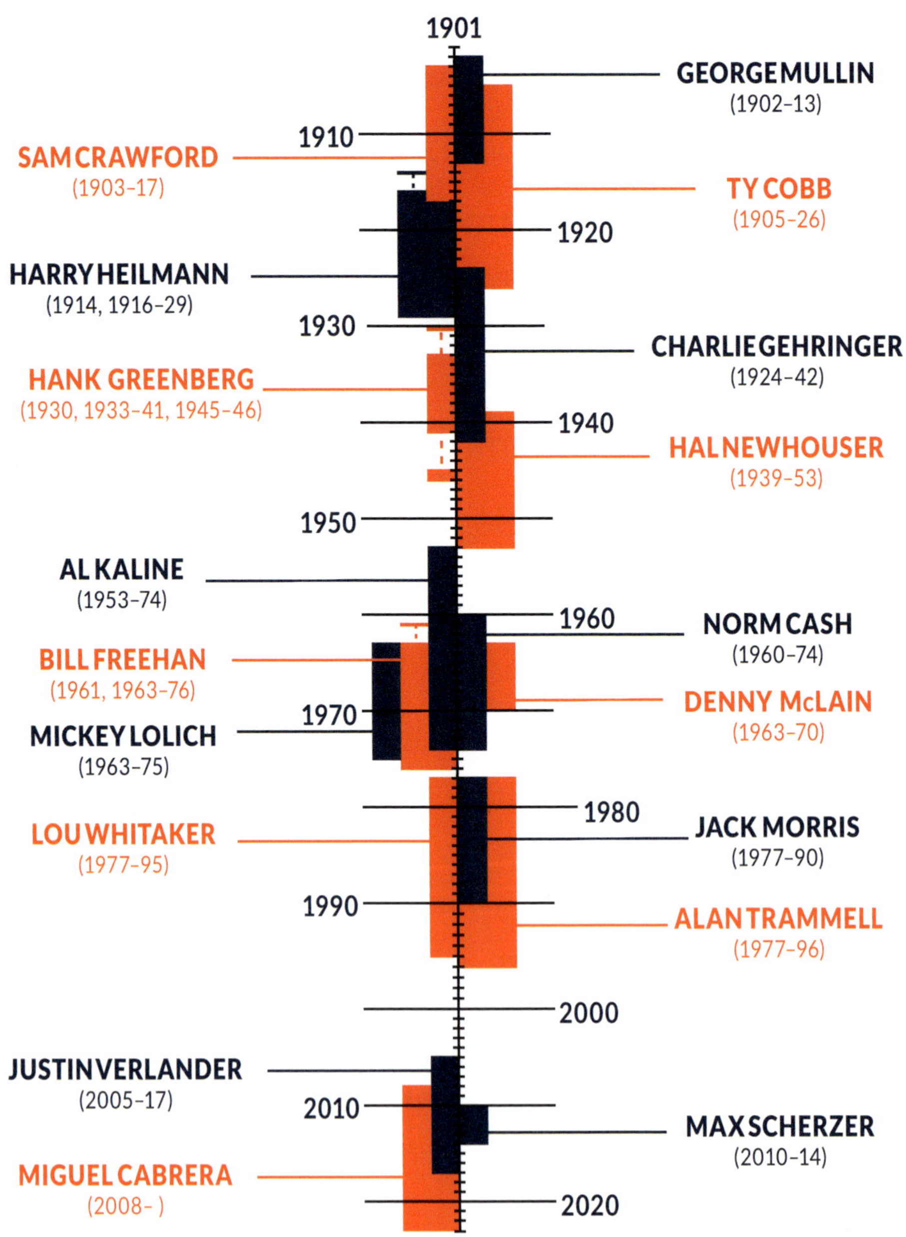

TEAM FACTS

DETROIT TIGERS

Founded: 1901

World Series titles: 4 (1935, 1945, 1968, 1984)*

Key managers:

Sparky Anderson (1979–95)

1,331–1,248–1 (.516), 1 World Series title

Mickey Cochrane (1934–38)

348–250–2 (.582), 1 World Series title

Jim Leyland (2006–13)

700–597 (.540)

MORE INFORMATION

To learn more about the Detroit Tigers, go to **pressboxbooks.com/AllAccess**.

These links are routinely monitored and updated to provide the most current information available.

through 2022

GLOSSARY

complete game
When one pitcher throws every inning in a single game.

debut
To make a first appearance.

elite
The best of the best.

pennant
A banner earned by the team that is the champion of the American League or National League each year.

perfect game
A game in which a pitcher doesn't allow any batters to reach base.

prospect
A player that people expect to do well at a higher level.

slump
A period when a team or player isn't performing up to expectations.

versatile
Able to do many different things.

INDEX